Planet Earth

THE BIG BANG AND BEYOND

MICHAEL BRIGHT

PowerKiDS press

Published in 2018 by **The Rosen Publishing Group, Inc.**
29 East 21st Street, New York, NY 10010

Cataloging-in-Publication Data

Names: Bright, Michael.
Title: The big bang and beyond / Michael Bright.
Description: New York : PowerKids Press, 2018. | Series: Planet Earth | Includes index.
Identifiers: ISBN 9781508153955 (pbk.) | ISBN 9781508153894 (library bound) | ISBN 9781508153788 (6 pack)
Subjects: LCSH: Big bang theory--Juvenile literature. | Cosmology--Juvenile literature. | Cosmogony--Juvenile literature.
Classification: LCC QB991.B54 B69 2018 | DDC 523.1'8--dc23

Written by Michael Bright
Cover illustration by Mark Turner
Editor: Corinne Lucas
Designer: Grant Kempster

Picture credits: p4 © AstroStar/Shutterstock; p5 © NASA, ESA, and the Hubble Heritage Team (AURA/STScI) (l); p5 © shooarts/Shutterstock (r); p6 © Amanda Carden/Shutterstock; p7 © NASA/Goddard (l); p7 © omepl1/Shutterstock (r); p8 © ISAS/JAXA; p9 © Vadim Sadovski/Shutterstock; p10 © National Geographic Creative/Alamy Stock Photo; p11 © Johan Swanepoel/Alamy Stock Photo (t); p11 © RICHARD BIZLEY/SCIENCE PHOTO LIBRARY (b); p12 © NASA/Don Davis (l); p12 © Romolo Tavani/Shutterstock (r); p12–13 © Roger Zhang/Shutterstock; p13 © Josef Hanus/Shutterstock (t); p13 © Jay Yuan/Shutterstock (m); p13 © Radius Images/Corbis (b); p14 © Kuttelvaserova Stuchelova/Shutterstock; p15 © Robert Crow/Shutterstock (t); p15 © Johan Swanepoel/Shutterstock (b); p16 © Mopic/Shutterstock; p17 © Arsgera/Shutterstock (t); p17 © robin2/Shutterstock (m); p17 © ChinaFotoPress/Contributor/Getty (b); p18 © Elena Kalistratova/Shutterstock; p18–19 © elnavegante/Shutterstock; p19 © mik ulyannikov/Shutterstock; p20 © Fesus Robert/Shutterstock; p21 © Martin Rietze/Westend61/Corbis (l); p21 © Bruno Ismael Silva Alves/Shutterstock (r); p23 © Andrey Yurlov/Shutterstock; p24 © Science Photo Library/Alamy Stock Photo; p24–25 © Boris-B/Shutterstock; p25 © Kazakova Maryia/Shutterstock; p26 © CLAUS LUNAU/SCIENCE PHOTO LIBRARY; p27 © CHRISTIAN DARKIN/SCIENCE PHOTO LIBRARY (t); p27 © SCIENCE PHOTO LIBRARY (b); p28 © Triff/Shutterstock (t); p28 © Yury Dmitrienko/Shutterstock (b); p28–9 © 360b/Shutterstock; p29 © Claudio Divizia/Shutterstock (1); p29 © pixelparticle/Shutterstock (2); p29 © Giraphics/Shutterstock (3); p29 © xpixel/Shutterstock (4); p29 © Bereziuk/Shutterstock (5). Background images and other graphic elements courtesy of Shutterstock.com.

Manufactured in China
CPSIA Compliance Information: Batch #BS17PK: For Further Information contact Rosen Publishing, New York, New York at 1-800-237-9932.

contents

origin of the
UNIVERSE

In the beginning was the Big Bang. Despite its name, it was not a great explosion, but the sudden appearance of the universe 13.8 **billion** years ago. At first, it was very small and extremely compact — no bigger than the period at the end of this sentence — but it immediately grew to an immense size at an unbelievable speed, maybe even faster than the speed of light.

cosmic dark ages

The early universe was dark. There were no stars. Scientists call it the **Cosmic** Dark Ages, but it was a special time in the story of Earth because the ingredients were gathering to make the first stars.

Stars made the basic chemicals that make us!

first stars

The first stars were massive chemical factories. Many of the chemicals that make up our world — including our own bodies — were **forged** inside of these stars. When they eventually exploded as gigantic **supernovae**, their chemicals were flung across the universe. These were the seeds of more stars that formed the first **galaxies**.

cosmic dust

Each supernova produced vast quantities of tiny, soot-like and sand-like chemical particles. A single explosion produced enough of this cosmic dust to make 7,000 Earths. It spread out in huge clouds in the space between stars, and into our spiral-shaped galaxy, the Milky Way. One supernova's cloud created our Sun, solar system, and planet Earth.

how do we know?

The Big Bang is a **theory**, not fact, but there is evidence that it is a possible explanation for the origins of the universe. By observing stars in distant parts of the universe from the **Hubble Space Telescope**, astronomers can see that galaxies are moving away from us. This indicates that the universe is expanding. It also means that 13.8 billion years ago, everything must have been closer together. Before the Big Bang, the universe was so squashed up that it was no bigger than a dot. After the Big Bang, everything expanded.

BIG BANG THEORY
metric expansion of space

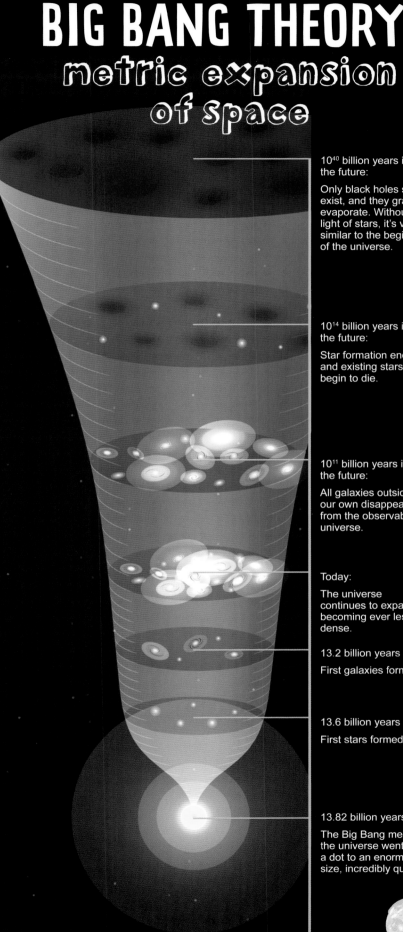

10^{40} billion years in the future:

Only black holes still exist, and they gradually evaporate. Without the light of stars, it's very similar to the beginning of the universe.

10^{14} billion years in the future:

Star formation ends, and existing stars begin to die.

10^{11} billion years in the future:

All galaxies outside our own disappear from the observable universe.

Today:

The universe continues to expand, becoming ever less dense.

13.2 billion years ago:

First galaxies formed.

13.6 billion years ago:

First stars formed.

13.82 billion years ago:

The Big Bang meant the universe went from a dot to an enormous size, incredibly quickly.

THE SUN

The Sun is a yellow dwarf star. It's about 93 million miles (150 million km) away from Earth, at the center of our solar system. It is the most important source of energy for life on Earth, because plants need sunlight to grow, and humans and other animals need plants to survive.

Core: where all the heat and light energy is generated.

Radiative zone: moves the heat rapidly to the **convection** zone.

Convection zone: moves the heat very slowly to the photosphere.

Photosphere: the Sun's surface, where light is released.

Chromosphere: a layer of gas above the Sun's surface that glows red.

Corona: the crown-like layer that's seen during a total eclipse.

Solar prominences: giant loops and fountains in the corona.

born in the Milky Way

The Sun was "born" 4.6 billion years ago, 5 billion years after the peak of star formation. During the peak, stars formed 30 times faster than they do today! By the time the Sun came into existence, the formation of stars in the Milky Way galaxy had already slowed to a trickle.

slow release

The temperature at the Sun's core is about 26,000,000° F (15,000,000° C) but all that heat takes several thousand years to work its way to the Sun's surface. Yet it only takes about 8 minutes and 20 seconds for the heat to reach Earth!

ball of plasma

The Sun's diameter is 109 times greater than that of Earth! It is mainly composed of hydrogen and helium gases, but it is not the same all the way through. The Sun has several different layers.

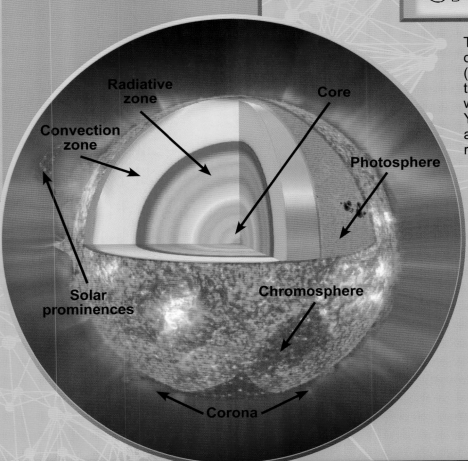

Radiative zone

Convection zone

Core

Photosphere

Solar prominences

Chromosphere

Corona

SYMBOL OF LIGHT

Ancient **civilizations** worshiped the Sun. It was hailed as the source of life, giving warmth and light for humankind. The ancient Romans put aside one day of the week to pray at dawn to the Sun god. This is where the modern day Sunday comes from.

ORIGIN of the solar system

The Sun and our solar system formed in a vast cloud of gas and dust in space. The cloud began to rotate and flattened into a disc. Most of the material was pulled to the center of the disc, forming our Sun. The remaining material in the disc eventually gathered together to form the planets, including Earth.

rocky planet formation

The tiny particles of dust in the disc smashed and joined together into small clumps. They then collided with other clumps and gradually grew in size. They became **asteroids** that were over a half a mile (1 km) across! They joined and formed larger bodies called **planetesimals**. These slammed into each other to form **protoplanets**, and these eventually became true planets, like planet Earth.

staggered creation

The planets formed at different times and are made up in different ways. The **gas giants**, Jupiter and Saturn, are composed mainly of hydrogen and helium gases. They were probably the first planets to form from the disc. The **ice giants**, Uranus and Neptune, contain frozen methane and **ammonia**. They were next to form. The smaller, rocky planets — Mercury, Venus, Earth, and Mars — were last.

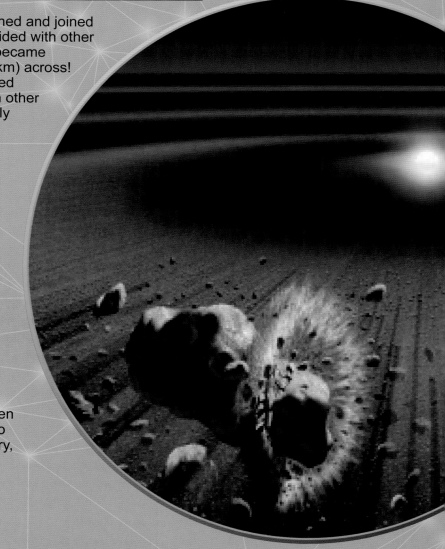

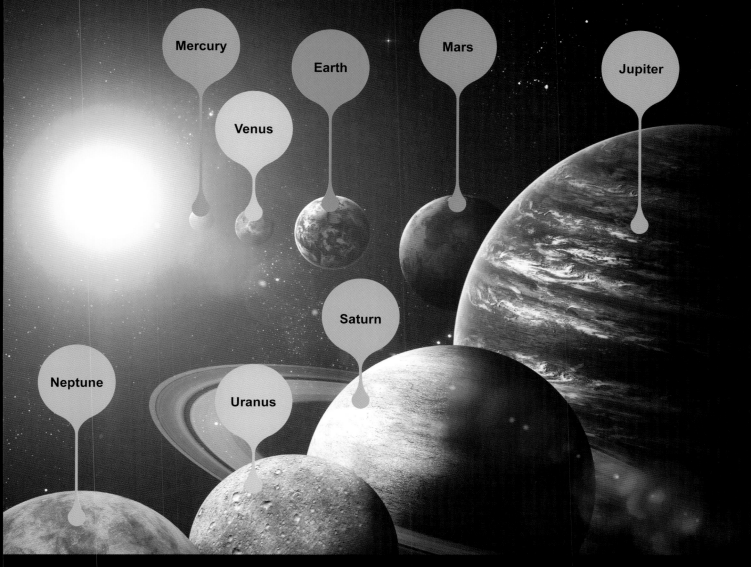

Mercury

Venus

Earth

Mars

Jupiter

Saturn

Neptune

Uranus

the solar system

After this chaotic start, the planets eventually settled into their current **orbits** around the Sun. The planets and other celestial objects in our solar system are vastly different from one another. Each has its own distinct and remarkable features:

Mercury's surface is covered in wrinkles! When the planet's iron core cooled and contracted, its rock formed wrinkles called Lobate Scarps.

Venus is nearly identical to Earth in size, chemistry, gravity, and density — but its very atmosphere would kill humans. Its high levels of carbon dioxide make it impossible for living things to survive.

Earth is the only known planet to have liquid water on its surface. Scientists think Jupiter's moon, Europa, might have liquid water under its solid surface.

Jupiter has a storm that has been raging just south of its equator for at least 340 years! We call it the Great Red Spot.

Saturn is known for its massive rings. They're made up of dust and chunks of ice and rock — some are as big as mountains!

Uranus is one of the ice giants, and it's the coldest planet in our solar system.

Neptune has a Great Dark Spot with winds blowing at 1,300 miles per hour (2,092 km/h).

The **asteroid belt** is made up of debris left over from the formation of the solar system.

The **Kuiper belt** contains the dwarf planet Pluto, asteroids, and small ice bodies.

The **Oort cloud** contains small, icy bodies at the edge of the solar system.

Planet Nine is a planet that scientists believe exists beyond Neptune - but we have not found it yet!

origin of EARTH

The Earth had a violent birth. After large asteroids crashed together to form most of the planet, many comets and meteorites continued to rain down on Earth from space, creating oceans of glowing, spitting, molten rock all over its surface.

calm intervals

Amongst the turmoil, scientists believe that by about 4 billion years ago the young Earth entered a brief period of calm, during which life might have evolved. The cooling of Earth caused rocks to solidify and **water vapor** in the **atmosphere** to form thick clouds. Rain from the clouds filled the first oceans and it's here that the first life-forms could have appeared. But these early seas would not have lasted long…

brutal bombardment

After Earth was formed, asteroids continued to smash into our planet. The impact of an incoming asteroid 400 miles (650 km) across would have caused all the water in the oceans to boil away. Even so, as long as the first tiny living things could hide from these collisions, deep underground or in other places, they could have survived.

god of the underworld

The first **geological** period on Earth is called the Hadean period, after Hades, the Greek god of the **underworld**. It lasted for about 500 million years, from Earth's origins to about 4 billion years ago. It was marked by the heavy bombardment of the planet by rocks from space and intense volcanic activity, alternating with periods of relative calm.

EARTH BORN TWICE

Some scientists believe that the Earth we live on today is not the original Earth. They think that the first Earth was a giant planet, but it was partly destroyed when Jupiter and Saturn moved towards the Sun and back out again. Scientists call this movement the "Grand Track" after the **maneuver** sailboats make when they turn. This may have created chaos in the early solar system, causing much of the first Earth to fall into the Sun. Scientists think the debris from the first Earth formed the Earth we know today. This would mean our Earth is much smaller than the original.

origin of the
MOON

Unlike many of the other planets in the solar system, which have up to 63 moons, Earth has only one. The Moon orbits Earth once every 27 days and is about 238,900 miles (384,400 km) away.

mysteries of the moon

One of science's greatest mysteries is how the Moon formed. It happened about 4.5 billion years ago, not long after Earth formed, but nobody can agree how. There are many theories, but two stand out from the rest.

GIANT IMPACT

This theory suggests that a space body the size of Mars, called Theia, crashed into Earth. Debris from the collision spun off and then clumped together to form the Moon.

NUCLEAR EXPLOSION

This theory proposes that a gigantic nuclear explosion went off close to the Earth's surface. It threw debris into space that formed the Moon. This is possible because several natural nuclear reactors existed in Oklo, Gabon, West Africa, and they were active about 1.5 billion years ago!

high tide

The Moon has an enormous influence on Earth. As it goes around our planet, it pulls the water in the oceans towards it, causing the tides. When the Sun lines up with the Moon, it adds to the pull, so we have extra high tides in the spring and the fall all over the world.

Bay of Fundy, North America

Home to the world's highest and lowest tides

SPIN OF THE EARTH

The distance of the Moon from Earth affects how fast Earth spins, but as it is moving away at about 1.5 inches (4 cm) per year, its influence is becoming gradually less. The result is that Earth is spinning more slowly and days are getting slightly longer than in the past. About 650 million years ago, a day lengthened by only 12 **microseconds** each year, but now it gets 23 microseconds longer each year!

EARTH
is like an onion

About a billion years ago, the innermost part of Earth's core turned solid. This was a very important moment in Earth's history. The heat flowing from the solid inner core caused the molten outer core to churn, creating Earth's **magnetic field**. The magnetic field has protected Earth for hundreds of millions of years from dangers in space and allowed life to begin and survive.

many layers

The inner core is now one of the several layers that make up Earth's interior. It was the most recent part to form.

earth's crust

The crust is a thin but solid skin that surrounds the planet and forms the continents and ocean floor. There are two types of crust. The oceanic crust is 3 miles (5 km) to 6 miles (10 km) thick and composed of dark rocks, such as basalt. The continental crust is 20 miles (30 km) to 30 miles (50 km) thick, consisting of lighter rocks, such as granite.

the core

The Earth's core is in two layers: a molten outer core and a more solid inner core. It is made of a mixture of elements, mainly iron and **nickel**, at a temperature of about 9,800° F (5,400° C). While the outer core remains molten, the intense pressure at the center has caused the inner core to "freeze," and it continues to freeze, growing by about 0.04 inch (1 mm) a year.

the mantle

The crust floats on the layer below, the mantle. The mantle appears to be solid but it actually behaves like a very thick and slow-moving liquid. It is about 1,793 miles (2,886 km) thick and has two zones, an upper and lower zone. Where the zones blend there is thought to be up to three times the amount of water locked up in the rocks than in all of the world's oceans put together.

DYNAMIC earth

The ground beneath our feet might seem to be still, but it's constantly moving. This is because the Earth's crust and **upper mantle** are divided up into segments, known as **tectonic plates**. They grow and shrink and move against each other, like a giant moving jigsaw puzzle. They form the continents and ocean floor, and have been moving since not long after Earth formed. It means that millions of years ago the oceans and continents had different shapes and locations than they do today.

plate boundaries

The boundaries between plates are geologically very active regions of the world. There are boundaries where plates are being formed, such as the Mid-Atlantic Ridge — which is the world's longest mountain chain and runs along the floor of the Atlantic Ocean. There are also places where they are being destroyed, such as the rim of the Pacific Ocean. These active regions are where most of the world's volcanoes erupt, earthquakes rumble and huge ocean waves, called **tsunamis**, race out across the ocean.

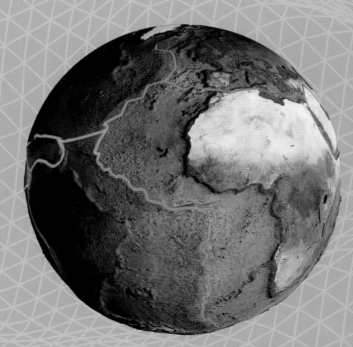

mountain building

Where one plate pushes against its neighbor and starts to buckle, huge mountain chains form, such as the Himalayas. The Himalayas are one of Earth's youngest mountain ranges and are home to the world's highest mountain, Mt. Everest, which stands 29,035 feet (8,850 m) above sea level.

ocean trenches

Where one plate is forced down below its neighbor, it is destroyed and ocean trenches form. These are the deepest parts of the ocean. The very deepest is the Mariana Trench, which has a maximum depth of 36,201 feet (11,034 m) below sea level.

SUPERCONTINENTS

About 300 million years ago, all the continents were joined together in one gigantic supercontinent, which scientists call Pangaea. About 175 million years ago, it began to split apart into two smaller supercontinents. These then broke up to form the continents we see today. Pangaea was not the only single supercontinent in Earth's history and it is unlikely to be the last. One day in the distant future all the continents are likely to join together, and the cycle will start again.

Eurasia

North America

Africa

South America

India

Antarctica

earth's early ATMOSPHERES

Today, Earth's atmosphere is made of nitrogen (78%), oxygen (21%), and tiny amounts of other gases, such as water vapor and carbon dioxide, but it was not always this way. The atmosphere has changed many times since Earth formed, and each change has had a huge impact on Earth.

gas exchange

Earth's first atmosphere was made of hydrogen and helium from the gas and dust cloud that formed the solar system. Much of it was lost to space, but as Earth cooled, volcanoes added more gases to the atmosphere. By then, it was mainly composed of carbon dioxide, water vapor, and smaller amounts of ammonia.

tropical heatwave

Carbon dioxide and water vapor are greenhouse gases — they trap heat like glass in a greenhouse, causing the greenhouse effect. This meant that even though the Sun was 30% less bright than it is today, the early Earth was very warm. That heat came partly from the Sun, and partly from the center of Earth. It meant that the air temperature, even during calm spells between asteroid bombardments, was a sizzling 158°F (70°C). This is about the same as the hottest place on Earth today — the Lut Desert in Iran, which has recorded a surface temperature of 159.3°F (70.7°C).

big cold

When life appeared, the atmosphere changed. Carbon dioxide levels went down because living things, such as plant-like bacteria, were taking in the gas for **photosynthesis**. Oxygen levels went up, partly because oxygen is produced during photosynthesis. This had a dramatic affect on Earth. With less greenhouse gas and a weak Sun, the planet cooled so much that it created the Huronian ice age. The Huronian ice age is the earliest and longest known ice age in Earth's history. It started about 2.4 billion years ago, and it lasted for 300 million years!

The Earth was frozen but life survived.

SNOWBALL EARTH

About 650 million years ago, the planet cooled so much that almost the entire surface was covered in ice or slush. The trigger could have been the eruption of a super-volcano whose dust blotted out the Sun, but nobody is sure. Scientists have called it "Snowball Earth" and they believe that somehow it triggered the sudden development of **multicelled** animals on Earth.

LIGHTNING
strike

Ever since our planet was formed, thunderstorms and lightning have been a prominent and often scary feature of the weather. Violent electrical storms probably accompanied the frequent volcanic eruptions on the surface of the early Earth. Across the world today there are up to 50 lightning flashes per second, each bolt lasting just 0.2 seconds.

electrical storms

Thunderstorms take place inside clouds of ash billowing from volcanoes, and where warm, moist air meets cold, dry air in the atmosphere. During a storm, lightning is the high-voltage release of electricity between clouds or between clouds and the ground. It superheats the air to 36,000° F (20,000° C) — more than three times the temperature of the Sun's surface — causing the sound of thunder.

prehistoric lightning

On the early Earth, lightning could have provided the energy needed to kick-start life. In a famous experiment in a laboratory, the ingredients of Earth's early oceans were put into a flask and zapped with artificial lightning. It produced some of the basic chemicals that make up living things.

lightning and life

Nitrogen is a vital chemical for life, but nitrogen as a gas does not react easily with other chemicals. It must be transformed into another form before living things can use it. Lightning can make that change. With up to 2,000 thunderstorms a day on today's Earth, and far more in earlier times, lightning has been an important producer of some of the chemicals used by living things to live and grow.

LIGHTNING AND FIRE

Lightning could have provided the first source of fire for prehistoric humans, before we could make it by striking flints together. Lightning caused wildfires or bushfires, from which early humans could have taken fire for their camps. In prehistoric times, it is likely that animals were caught in the bushfires, and when early humans scavenged their meat, it could have been their first taste of cooked food.

CLIMATE change

Climate change and global warming have been in the news a lot in recent years. The concern is that man-made **pollution**, particularly carbon dioxide from burning oil, coal or natural gas, is causing Earth's air and sea temperatures to rise due to the greenhouse effect. Looking into Earth's past, scientists can find times when this occurred naturally, and see if something similar might happen today.

Dinosaurs arose in a warming world.

Earth's stormy future.

dinosaur greenhouse

About 200 million years ago, massive volcanic eruptions poured enormous amounts of carbon dioxide into the atmosphere, trapping heat from a hotter Sun than today, to trigger a global rise in temperature. This caused a special chemical ice on the seabed to melt, releasing another powerful greenhouse gas, methane. Life was under threat from this rapidly warming world, and half of all creatures on land and in the sea became extinct. The way was open for a group of animals that somehow escaped the devastation to take over the world — the dinosaurs!

naturally warming world

About 55.8 million years ago, a huge amount of carbon found its way into the atmosphere and the average global temperature rose by about 9° F (5° C). The climate became unstable all over the world and great storms raged, each lasting for more than a thousand years. The cause of this **Paleocene-Eocene** Thermal Maximum (PETM), as it is known, is a puzzle but some animals benefited from the change, while others died out. One group that took advantage were our immediate ancestors — the early primates.

A WARNING FROM THE PAST

Scientists believe something similar to the PETM could happen to Earth's climate in the near future because they predict a global temperature rise of as much as 11.5° F (6.4° C) by the end of the 21st century. Arctic and Antarctic ice would melt, the oceans would become acidic, sea levels would rise, and storms would batter Earth. But which animal would survive the changes and take over the world this time?

earth's
WATER

One thing that sets Earth apart from all the other planets in the solar system is the large quantities of liquid water on its surface and water vapor in its atmosphere. Scientists believe Earth was creating oceans not long after it formed, about 4.4 billion years ago.

triple sources

Earth's water probably arrived in three ways. Up to half came from the cloud of gas and dust that formed the solar system. This water is older than the Sun. Water was also locked away in Earth's rocks and eventually reached the surface during major geological events, such as volcanic eruptions. Lastly, some might have come from space via asteroids and comets, during the bombardment of the early Earth.

FOSSIL WATER

The length of time water is held in different parts of the water cycle varies. Water can be in the atmosphere for nine days, a river for six months, a **glacier** for 100 years, and held underground for 10,000 years, where it is known as fossil water.

Salt water and fresh

Today, the planet's water is divided into several categories: the freshwater of lakes, rivers, and **groundwater**, the frozen water of **ice caps** and glaciers, the salt water of seas and oceans, water vapor in the atmosphere, and the water in living things. It covers 71% of Earth's surface and about 96.5% of it is in the oceans.

water cycle

Earth's water is constantly on the move. The water **evaporates** from oceans, and rises as water vapor in columns of warm air. It cools and changes back to a liquid as water droplets that attach to dust particles to form clouds. The clouds are moved along by the wind towards the land, where they drop the water as rain or snow. The rain runs off the land into rivers and eventually flows back into the sea, where the cycle starts all over again.

blue
PLANET

Most of Earth's water is salt water. Today, it is contained in five oceans and countless seas, gulfs, and bays, but it was not always this way. About 300 million years ago there was only one ocean surrounding the supercontinent of Pangaea. This "superocean" was called Panthalassa, and it eventually gave rise to the Pacific Ocean.

oceans come and go

When Pangaea broke apart into the two smaller supercontinents, Gondwana and Laurasia, the Tethys Sea formed between them, creating a continuous belt of water running around Earth to the north of the **Equator**. With no continents in the way, the Tethys Sea must have been very stormy, like the Southern Ocean is today.

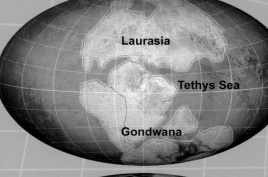

marine mountain

While the Atlantic and Indian oceans were forming, the seabed of the Tethys Sea was pushed high into the air, and when India bumped into the rest of Asia, it formed the Himalayas. Now, you can find fossils of sea creatures in rocks on the top of Mt. Everest!

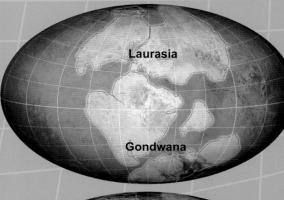

Earth at the time of Pangea.

growing atlantic

When the two supercontinents also broke up, the continents we know today began to move around. They opened up the Indian Ocean, but closed the Tethys Sea. Some of the Tethys formed the Atlantic Ocean, the part from the Mediterranean to the Caribbean. The rest of the Atlantic formed when North and South America parted company with Europe and Africa, first creating the North Atlantic and then the South Atlantic.

oceans today

Today, the largest ocean is the Pacific Ocean, with the Atlantic and Indian oceans second and third. The Arctic Ocean is covered by ice in winter, and the turbulent Southern Ocean flows around Antarctica, similar to how the Tethys Sea flowed around Earth millions of years ago.

Global ocean circulation. Red is warm currents and blue is cold.

HABITABLE
planet

The chemistry of life probably began not long after the Big Bang, and it is possible that microscopic life-forms exist throughout the universe. There are thought to be more than 11 billion Earth-sized planets in the Milky Way, which are orbiting Sun-like stars. Yet Earth is the only place we know that has life. What makes our planet so special?

A life-supporting planet must have a source of energy, such as a star like the Sun. The star must not vary too much or too quickly, or life would not have a chance to grow.

There must not be a large gas giant planet nearby to disrupt the formation of an Earth-like space body. In the solar system, the presence of Jupiter stops the debris in the asteroid belt from clumping together to form a planet. If it had been located between Venus and Mars, Earth might never have formed.

The planet must have a moon that helps steady the way it tilts towards its star. The stabilizing affect of Earth's Moon could be one reason why there is life on Earth.

The planet must be the right distance from its star to be at the right temperature for liquid water. But this does not mean that water is necessary for all forms of life.

The planet must be able to keep an atmosphere, and it should rotate reasonably quickly so that day and night are not too long.

It must be a rocky planet that is geologically alive with tectonic plates, volcanoes and earthquakes. These keep the planet supplied with the essential chemicals for life. It must also have an iron core for a magnetic field to shield it from anything harmful in space.

The planet must have the right mix of chemicals, and be able to assemble and maintain the very complex molecules that function as life.

glossary

ammonia a chemical compound of nitrogen and hydrogen

asteroid a space rock ranging in size from 0.6 to 578 miles (1 km to 930 km), found circling the Sun between the orbits of Mars and Jupiter

atmosphere the layer of gases around a planet

billion a thousand million

civilization a particular group of people at a particular time

climate weather conditions over a long period

convection heat transfer in a gas or liquid by circulating currents, like a pot of boiling water

cosmic relating to the universe

Eocene the geological time span from 56 to 33.9 million years ago

Equator an imaginary line that circles around Earth halfway between the North and South poles

evaporate to change from a liquid to a gas

forge to give form or shape to something

galaxies collections of stars

gas giant a very large planet made mainly of gas rather than rocks, such as Jupiter

geological reference to the science that studies the origin, history and structure of Earth

glacier a solid river of ice

groundwater water kept in the ground or in natural underground reservoirs

Hubble Space Telescope a telescope on a satellite circling Earth

ice cap a permanent area of ice and snow over the land

ice giant a very large planet made partly of frozen chemicals, such as methane

magnetic field an invisible force that surrounds Earth, which is like a bar magnet with a north and a south

maneuver a movement or series of movements requiring skill

microsecond one-millionth of a second

molten made liquid with heat

multicelled having a body made of more than one cell

nickel a silvery, hard, metallic element

orbit the path of a planet, asteroid or comet around a star, or a moon around a planet

Paleocene the geological time span from 66 to 56 million years ago

photosynthesis the process by which green plants convert sunlight, water and carbon dioxide into sugars, and emit oxygen

planetesimal a space rock with its own gravity that might form into a planet

pollution a harmful substance introduced to the environment

protoplanet the stage of planet formation before a true planet

supernovae exploding stars

tectonic plate a slab of solid rock on Earth's surface, which can be a continent or the ocean floor, that floats on the Earth's mantle

theory an idea based on good observation that has yet to be proven as fact

tsunami a gigantic wave in the sea that is caused by earth movements, such as an earthquake

underworld a mythical world of the dead under the ground

upper mantle the layer of Earth between the outer crust and the lower mantle

water vapor the gas form of water

Books

Big Bang! The Tongue-Tickling Tale of a Speck that Became Spectacular (2005)
Carolyn Cinami DeCristofano and Michael Carroll
Charlesbridge Publishing

Older Than the Stars (2011)
Karen C. Fox and Nancy Davis
Charlesbridge Publishing

*Born with a Bang: The Universe Tells Our Cosmic Story,
Sharing Nature with Children Book* (2002)
Jennifer Morgan and Dana Lynne Andersen
Dawn Publications

Encyclopedia of Planet Earth (2013)
Anna Claybourne
Usborne Publishing

Watch This Space: The Universe, Black Holes, and the Big Bang (2015)
Clive Gifford
Wayland

Websites

PowerKids Press has developed an online list of websites related to the subject of this book. This site is updated regularly. Please use this link to access the list:
www.powerkidslinks.com/pe/bigbang

index